The Landscape of Dartm

£1
5/22

The Landscape of Dartmoor

AMBASSADOR

SALMON

Published by J Salmon Limited
100 London Road, Sevenoaks, Kent TN13 1BB

First edition 1999

Designed by the Salmon Studio

Copyright © 1999 J Salmon Limited

ISBN 1 898435 82 0

Printed in England by
J Salmon Limited, Tubs Hill Works, Sevenoaks, Kent

Front cover: Bowerman's Nose
Back cover: A Dartmoor Cross
Half title page: From Peekhill
Title page: Postbridge
Facing page: Steps Bridge

Introduction

Dartmoor covers about 130,000 acres and measures some 22 miles from north to south and 14 miles from east to west, with an average height of between 1,500 and 1,600 feet. It is southern England's last untamed wilderness and the essential heartland of Devon, the cradle of its rivers and the haunt of its legends.

The general features of the moor are those of a wild upland, with peat for its soil, and crowned on the heights by granite tors of fantastic shapes. Its moods depend upon the sun and the clouds in the most remarkable manner. When the blanket of mist descends on the scene nothing could be more desolate. Spectral rocks appear for a moment and then seem to glide out of sight; away from the main roads tenacious bogs await the unwary walker. But when the sky clears the whole surroundings undergo a marvellous transformation. The granite throws aside its dull grey tints and assumes an almost prismatic radiance. The play of colour over the shoulders of the moor alters with delightful abruptness from the purples of the heather to the yellow of the gorse and the metallic green of the whortle.

Not unfrequently, a herd of Dartmoor ponies are seen; shaggy, sure-footed little beasts with wills of their own, even after they have been broken in. In the heart of the moor wild animal life, though fairly abundant, is secretive. The foxes and badgers are shy about showing themselves, but it occasionally happens that one of the rarer hawks can be seen hovering over its destined prey.

Over the whole face of the moor traces of ancient Celtic occupation abound in the shape of stone circles, menhirs and village enclosures. The eeriness of the landscape is accentuated by the lych or ancient trackways and the stone rows, of which there are thirty-eight long avenues of ancient stones usually leading from a stone circle containing a barrow to a menhir, a single, upright stone. The row that leads to the Dancers of Styall Moor is two miles long.

◁ Dartmoor ponies

The finest circles are at Scorhill and Fernworthy; the highest menhir, nearly 18 feet, is at Drizzlecombe. The best hut-circle is at Grimspound, which is bounded by walls about four feet high and encloses twenty-four hut-circles within its four acres, where a prehistoric village of the Early Bronze Period once stood.

At the time of the Norman conquest Dartmoor became a royal hunting domain, abounding in red deer and wolves. Subsequently, under Edward I, large parts were united with the Duchy of Cornwall as lands of the Prince of Wales. Certain customs and rights still hold from these times. The moorfolk still hold "venville" rights over the forest which enables them to pasture their cattle, sheep, and ponies, cut turf, and take away sand and stones in return for assisting at the "drifts," a process of rounding-up the ponies.

The moorland streams are crossed by ancient "clapper" bridges, huge flat slabs of granite, supported by thicker slabs, that have been in position from time immemorial. Their unmortared weather-stained stones are coloured with lichen or moss, with banks of grass or heather, lapped by the clearest and coolest of mountain streams in summer, and lashed by torrents in rainy winter seasons. Old ruined blowing houses remind the wanderer of the tin-smelting days when miners held their own Stannary Parliament on Crockern Tor round a large granite slab which may still be seen at Dunnabridge Farm.

To the north and east the moor assumes a softer and more gentle face, around the valleys of the Teign and Bovey. Picturesque villages nestle among the slopes. Narrow lanes lead off in all directions, and which-ever you take you come on a fresh delight. There are quiet bathing pools under shady trees all along the amber-coloured rivers; there are dense woods on steep sides through which streams tumble over granite boulders; on the high slopes the white farms give evidence of man's endeavour to tame the moor's fringes.

Hound Tor ▷

Situated in the beautiful valley of the East Webburn River and surrounded by rolling hills, **Widecombe-in-the-Moor** is arguably the most famous village on Dartmoor. It is known for its annual fair, held in September, which was established about 150 years ago and is immortalised in the traditional song Widecombe Fair. The 15th century Church of St. Pancras is the second largest parish church in Devon and because of its great size this prominent landmark is known as the "Cathedral of the Moor". In the Middle Ages tin-mining was important to the economy of the area and the tower of Widecombe's church was paid for, in part, by local miners.

◁ The Green, Widecombe-in-the-Moor
Widecombe-in-the-Moor ▷

One of the most famous beauty spots on the moor is at **Dartmeet** where the East and West Dart rivers flow into each other and start their beautifully wooded descent towards Buckfastleigh on the south eastern edge of Dartmoor. Here a clapper bridge, thought to date from the 13th century, crosses the boulder-strewn river a little way upstream of the modern bridge. It is constructed with huge blocks of stone, a method of bridge building which is common on Dartmoor where large slabs of rock are readily available. From Dartmeet there are fine walks along the valley of the **West Dart River** which rises in the uplands in the northern part of the moor. Near Hexworthy the river is spanned by the elegant Huccaby Bridge.

◁ Dartmeet
Huccaby Bridge ▷

There are numerous pretty little streams which wind like threads across the high moorland of the Dartmoor National Park. Rising in the hills in the heart of the moor the **East Dart River** twists and turns on its way southwards through a narrow, steep gorge until it joins the West Dart River at Dartmeet where the river is known as Double Dart. Some four miles north of this point, at **Postbridge**, the East Dart River is spanned by one of Dartmoor's ancient clapper bridges. Built of huge granite slabs supported on four piers, it is the largest of the clapper bridges on the moor at over forty feet in length and for many centuries provided the main crossing point on the river. This medieval bridge was probably built for the use of pack horses travelling from the tin mines to the Stannary towns of Tavistock and Chagford. On a slope about a mile from the hamlet of Postbridge there is a group of prehistoric hut circles and from this site there is a splendid view of the East Dart Valley.

◁ Near Postbridge
Postbridge ▷

Crockern Tor, which reaches an impressive height of 1,391 feet, is situated near the hamlet of Two Bridges in the heart of Dartmoor's former tin mining country. This bleak and exposed spot is sometimes known as Parliament Rock for it was here over a period of many centuries that the Stannary Court, or "Tinners' Parliament" was held. Here the representatives of the stannary towns met to enact laws. Some two miles along the valley of the West Dart River above Two Bridges is **Wistman's Wood**, all that remains of Dartmoor's native oak forests. Here ancient gnarled and twisted oaks stand among scattered granite outcrops while mosses, lichens and ferns grow in profusion among the trees. The area is now a Nature Conservancy reserve.

◁ Crockern Tor
Wistman's Wood ▷

Haytor stands 1,490 feet above sea level and provides one of the finest viewpoints on Dartmoor taking in the South Devon coastline as well as the heather-covered moorland to the north. One of the best known of the many rocky outcrops scattered across the moor, these ancient rocks are much visited by holiday-makers and tourists all year round. It was from quarries nearby that granite was taken for such well-known buildings as the original London Bridge and the British Museum. In the first half of the nineteenth century the stone was transported in horse-drawn trucks along the Granite Tramway to a canal in the valley. The remains of the granite rails, grooved to hold the wooden wheels of the trucks, can still be seen.

◁ Haytor
The Granite Tramway, Haytor ▷

Contrasting with the austere granite moorland in the north of Dartmoor, the gentler eastern moor has deeply wooded valleys where picturesque villages nestle. A delightful cluster of thatched cottages stands in the little hamlet of **Ponsworthy** which is surrounded by trees and lush green meadows. Here a tiny watercourse runs across the road providing a popular subject for artists and photographers. The attractive small village of **Buckland-in-the-Moor** is little more than a cluster of picturesque thatched cottages, clinging to the steeply sloping banks of the River Dart. A unique feature of tiny Buckland Church is that, instead of numbers to mark the hours, the clock face bears letters which spell the words "My dear mother".

◁ Ponsworthy
Buckland-in-the-Moor ▷

Wild and remote Dartmoor is the largest remaining area of unspoilt moorland in southern England and here ponies have run wild on the moor for at least a thousand years. These sturdy animals, which are such a popular sight with visitors, roam freely across the rock-strewn, heather-clad moorland in all weathers finding shelter from the elements beneath the granite outcrops. Ponies are often seen grazing by the roadside and it has been made an offence to feed them as this attracts them onto the roads where they are in danger from passing traffic. The ponies are in fact owned by farmers for whom horse breeding, together with the rearing of sheep and cattle, is a traditional activity. Each autumn the ponies are rounded-up in spectacular drifts so that the foals can be branded, after which many of them are sold.

◁ Dartmoor Ponies ▷

The name 'tor' is derived from a Celtic word meaning tower and **Hound Tor**, like many of the other outcrops on the moor, is conspicuously sited on high ground. It stands north-east of famous Widecombe-in-the-Moor within sight of Haytor, another of the granite rock formations which the wind and rain have carved into curious shapes. The remains of a medieval village, once a busy moorland community, can be seen just east of Hound Tor. At the beauty spot of **Becky Falls**, near the moorland village of Manaton, the fast-running Becka Brook cascades 70 feet over boulders into a wooded glade. It is particularly impressive after heavy rain when water pours off the moor down a steep ravine. There are numerous footpaths through the surrounding woodland which enable ramblers to explore this enchanting valley.

◁ Hound Tor
Becky Falls ▷

The River Bovey rises, like the River Dart, as two separate streams and once they are united the river flows south-east across the moor into the River Teign and thence to the sea. The river valley embraces some delightful moorland villages such as **Lustleigh**, a village on the eastern edge of the Dartmoor National Park which seems to have withstood the passage of time. Renowned for its traditional May Day festivities, Lustleigh is clustered around its fine 13th century church and there are numerous ancient granite cottages with the deeply thatched roofs which are typical of this part of Devon. At nearby Lustleigh Cleave there is an especially attractive stretch of the river which has become a local beauty spot. Shortly before it joins the Teign, the River Bovey flows through **Bovey Tracey**, eastern gateway to Dartmoor and also within easy reach of the south Devon resorts of Teignmouth and Torbay. This attractive small town is noted for its fine church which is believed to have been built in honour of Thomas à Becket by the de Tracey family who gave their name to the town and whose ancestors were implicated in the murder of the saint.

◁ Lustleigh
Bovey Tracey ▷

Dartmoor is a land of rivers and all the great rivers of South Devon have their source here. From the uplands of the moor, the **River Teign** descends in a series of rapids and small waterfalls through some wild and beautiful scenery to its broad estuary some twenty-five miles away at Teignmouth. On its journey it is spanned by a number of picturesque bridges. **Steps Bridge** is situated near Dunsford, in the higher reaches of the lovely Teign Valley while **Fingle Bridge**, about four miles away to the south of Drewsteignton, is one of the most handsome of Dartmoor's many ancient bridges. It stands in one of the wildest and most beautiful parts of the steep-sided Fingle Gorge which was described by R. D. Blackmore, author of Lorna Doone, as the "finest scene in all England." Constructed in the time of Queen Elizabeth I, the bridge is now a popular place both with walkers and artists.

◁ Steps Bridge
Fingle Bridge ▷

One of the few remaining areas of natural, virgin land remaining in the south of England, Dartmoor is known for its rugged landscape. Among the numerous rocky outcrops which have been shaped by the elements is **Bowerman's Nose**, a distinctive 22 feet high pillar of weathered granite. One of Dartmoor's best known features, this striking rock stands on the moor near Manaton. About three miles to the north is **North Bovey**. Reputed to be one of the most beautiful villages in England, it stands on the slopes above the River Bovey offering splendid views across the wooded valley to the moors beyond. The village green, where an ancient cross has stood since medieval times, is surrounded by attractive thatched cottages and the church dates mainly from the 15th century.

◁ North Bovey
Bowerman's Nose ▷

An excellent centre for exploring the eastern part of Dartmoor, **Moretonhampstead** is a small market town with some fine old buildings. The church, with its handsome tower, is a prominent landmark and there are also some unusual two-storeyed almshouses which were built in 1637 from Dartmoor granite. Thatched, and with an open colonnade facing the road, these beautiful buildings are now owned by the National Trust. Near the town, the impressive Iron Age fort of Cranbrook Castle, constructed more than two thousand years ago, has a commanding view over the deep valley of the River Teign. Another of Dartmoor's delightful villages of granite and thatch, **Drewsteignton** is situated on a ridge above the River Teign gorge surrounded by some of the most beautiful wooded countryside that Dartmoor has to offer. At the heart of the village is the square with its inn, cottages and church. A lych-gate beside a tiny almshouse leads from the square into the churchyard.

◁ Drewsteignton
Moretonhampstead ▷

Situated almost in the centre of Devon, the small market town of **Chagford** makes an excellent centre for touring. It was one of the four ancient stannary towns where the tin-miners of Dartmoor would bring their tin to be weighed, assayed and sold. It lies amidst some of the most beautiful scenery in the National Park, with open moorland, wooded hills and the lovely Teign Valley all within easy reach. The picturesque and peaceful village of **Throwleigh** is situated on the northern edge of the moor between Chagford and Okehampton. Among the delights of Throwleigh's interesting little church is the ornate priest's doorway and the thatched lych-gate. Around it are grouped some beautiful cottages, the thatched Church House, which dates from early Tudor times, and the 18th century Old Parsonage. The village is surrounded by superb, unspoiled scenery and the nearby Throwleigh stone circle is one of the best monuments of its kind on the moor.

◁ Chagford
Throwleigh ▷

Dartmoor is rich in prehistoric relics and there is ample evidence that the area has been inhabited since the Bronze Age. The **Scorhill Stone Circle** – one of Dartmoor's finest prehistoric stone circles – stands in isolation high on the moor to the west of Chagford near the village of Gidleigh. Between Chagford and Drewsteignton is **Spinsters' Rock**, the only upright dolmen standing in Devon. It consists of a huge slab of stone, some fifteen feet by ten, which rests on three upright stones, each over six feet in height. This impressive monument dates from neolithic times and is thought to be the tomb of a local chieftain. It acquired its intriguing name from a legend that it was erected before breakfast by three exceptionally strong unmarried women.

◁ Scorhill Stone Circle
Spinster's Rock ▷

Okehampton is situated on the northern fringe of Dartmoor within reach of its two highest points, High Willhays and Yes Tor. Mentioned in the Domesday Book, this ancient town was one of only two market towns in the county at the time of the Norman conquest. Okehampton Castle, begun in William the Conqueror's time and added to in later centuries, was once one of the most powerful castles in the country and a substantial part still stands including the ruined chapel, keep and hall. Originally built to protect travellers, it stands on high ground beside the main route from Exeter to Cornwall. This same strategic position on the main route across central Devon made Okehampton important as a staging post in the days of the stagecoach.

◁ Okehampton Castle
Fore Street, Okehampton ▷

Once a Saxon fortress town but now a small village, Lydford is situated near the north-western boundary of the National Park. Extending for a mile and a half just south of the town is **Lydford Gorge**, a deep and dramatic ravine formed by the valley of the River Lyd. Here a magnificent waterfall, known as White Lady Waterfall, plunges 90 feet into the gorge through a thickly wooded landscape. Close by and offering extensive views over a large part of Devon and Cornwall, **Brentor** is a prominent local landmark on the western edge of the moor. This is not one of the granite tors which abound on Dartmoor but rather it is an isolated volcanic outcrop. According to legend, the 12th century Church of St. Michael which stands on the summit of the 1,130 feet high hill was built by a grateful merchant whose ship had narrowly escaped shipwreck. However, it may well have been the monks from Tavistock Abbey who were actually responsible for founding the church.

◁ Lydford Gorge
Brentor ▷

There are several hundred crosses on Dartmoor. Some stand in villages or churchyards marking sites which were used for preaching or as starting points for processions; some were put up as memorials or boundary markers; others indicate the route of ancient trackways such as The Abbot's Way linking Buckfast Abbey with Tavistock Abbey. Roughly hewn out of granite, these ancient crosses are now well weathered and have become part of the landscape of the moor. A well-known landmark high up on a desolate part of the moor near Princetown is **Dartmoor Prison**. Originally built to house French prisoners during the Napoleonic Wars, the prison was closed when the Battle of Waterloo brought an end to the war in 1815. Subsequently, when Australia refused to accept any more convicts, the prison was converted to provide secure accommodation for criminals, which it has done since 1850. Dominating this part of Dartmoor, the forbidding building is surrounded by fields and quarries in which the prisoners work.

◁ Dartmoor Cross
Dartmoor Prison ▷

The delightful little village of **Sheepstor** is situated about six miles north of Plymouth in the south-western corner of the moor. Sheltered beneath the tor which bears its name, it is surrounded by some of Dartmoor's loveliest scenery, a combination of moorland and cultivated fields lying at the foot of conifer-clad hills. Sheepstor's small granite church was re-built in the 15th century and here is buried the famous Rajah of Sarawak who lived at nearby Burrator, the site of Devon's largest and most attractive reservoir built in 1898 to serve the needs of the city of Plymouth. The area is rich in relics of the Bronze Age and there are numerous hut circles, cairns and stone circles scattered over the tors and hills which rise from the moors. Threading through the landscape is the charming River Meavy, a tributary of the Plym.

◁ River Meavy
Sheepstor ▷

Buckfast Abbey lies in a fertile valley beside the River Dart on the south-eastern edge of Dartmoor. It was a very early foundation of the Savigniac order and was well established by the reign of King Canute. In common with many other religious houses, it fell into ruin after the Dissolution of the Monasteries but in the 1880s the site was acquired by French Benedictine monks and the present magnificent structure was built on the original foundations. In modern times the monks of Buckfast have become famous for producing tonic wine as well as honey from their own hives. A few miles upstream, beautiful 15th century **Holne Bridge** spans the River Dart at a picturesque wooded spot where the riverside paths and beautiful scenery are best explored on foot. High above the west bank of the river is Holne Village with its fine church and here, in the vicarage, Charles Kingsley, author of The Water Babies and Westward Ho!, was born in 1819.

◁ River Dart near Holne
Buckfast Abbey ▷

Index